DOLPHINS SET I

SPOTTED DOLPHINS

Megan M. Gunderson
ABDO Publishing Company

visit us at
www.abdopublishing.com

Published by ABDO Publishing Company, 8000 West 78th Street, Edina, Minnesota 55439. Copyright © 2011 by Abdo Consulting Group, Inc. International copyrights reserved in all countries. No part of this book may be reproduced in any form without written permission from the publisher. The Checkerboard Library™ is a trademark and logo of ABDO Publishing Company.

Printed in the United States of America, North Mankato, Minnesota.
042010
092010

 PRINTED ON RECYCLED PAPER

Cover Photo: Photolibrary
Interior Photos: © Doug Perrine / SeaPics.com p. 18; Getty Images p. 5; National Geographic Stock pp. 8, 15; Peter Arnold pp. 13, 14, 21; Photolibrary p. 17; Uko Gorter pp. 7, 9

Editor: Tamara L. Britton
Art Direction & Cover Design: Neil Klinepier

Library of Congress Cataloging-in-Publication Data

Gunderson, Megan M., 1981-
  Spotted dolphins / Megan M. Gunderson.
      p. cm. -- (Dolphins)
  Includes index.
  ISBN 978-1-61613-415-0
  1. Atlantic spotted dolphin--Juvenile literature. I. Title.
  QL737.C432G8597 2010
  599.53'4--dc22
                                        2010001585

CONTENTS

SPOTTED DOLPHINS

Schools of hundreds of spotted dolphins live and play in Earth's warm, salty oceans. These speedy **cetaceans** are **warm-blooded** and nurse their young. Spotted dolphins surface to take air into their lungs. They breathe through a single blowhole at the top of the head.

Spotted dolphins are mammals from the family **Delphinidae**. Within that family, scientists have identified two spotted dolphin species. The first is the Atlantic spotted dolphin. The second is the pantropical spotted dolphin. The name *pantropical* means it lives in **tropical** areas around the world.

The amount of spots a spotted dolphin has depends partly on its age.

Size, Shape, and Color

In both species, male spotted dolphins are slightly larger than females. The average pantropical spotted male grows five to nine feet (1.6 to 2.6 m) in length. It weighs 198 to 262 pounds (90 to 119 kg).

The average Atlantic spotted male is shorter but heavier. It measures five to eight feet (1.6 to 2.3 m) long and weighs 220 to 315 pounds (100 to 143 kg).

The pantropical spotted has a slender body and a narrow beak. The Atlantic spotted has a stockier body and beak.

The Atlantic spotted has flippers that are curved and pointed. The pantropical spotted has smaller, tapered flippers. Its flukes are also smaller. And, it has the narrowest dorsal fin of any dolphin.

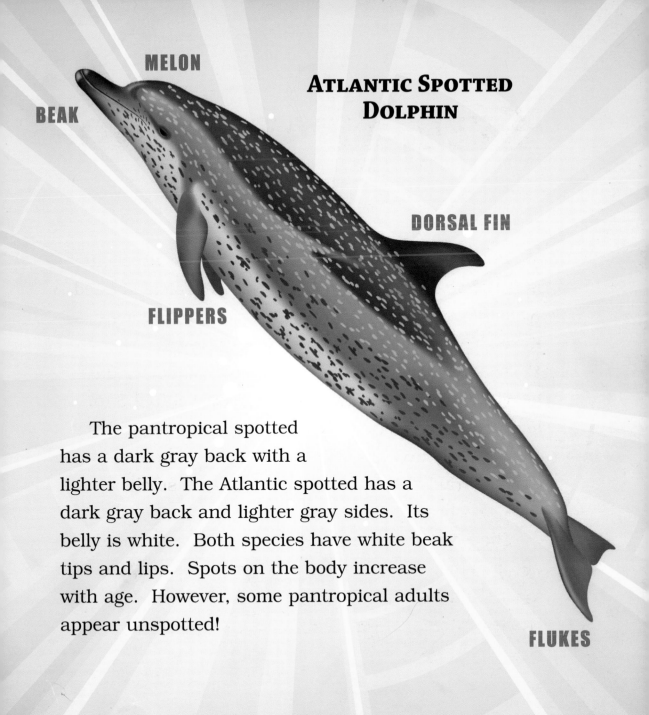

BEAK

MELON

ATLANTIC SPOTTED DOLPHIN

DORSAL FIN

FLIPPERS

The pantropical spotted
has a dark gray back with a
lighter belly. The Atlantic spotted has a
dark gray back and lighter gray sides. Its
belly is white. Both species have white beak
tips and lips. Spots on the body increase
with age. However, some pantropical adults
appear unspotted!

FLUKES

WHERE THEY LIVE

Spotted dolphins play with seaweed and other objects from their surroundings.

Spotted dolphins are found in **tropical** and warm **temperate** ocean waters. Atlantic spotted dolphins live only in the Atlantic Ocean. They prefer areas around coasts and **continental shelves**. However, they have also been seen far offshore.

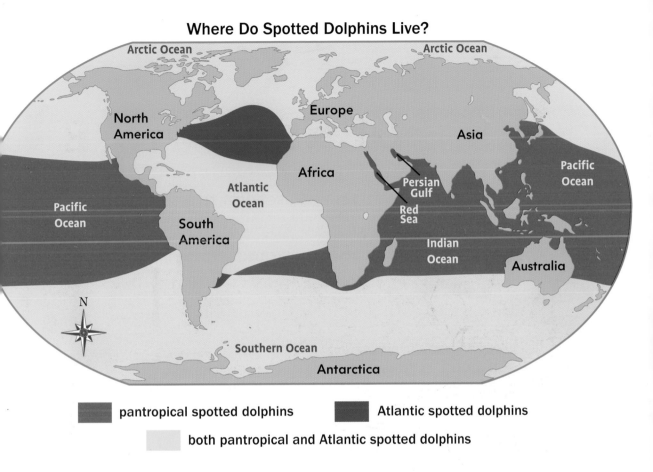

Where Do Spotted Dolphins Live?

- **pantropical spotted dolphins**
- **Atlantic spotted dolphins**
- **both pantropical and Atlantic spotted dolphins**

Pantropical spotted dolphins have a much larger range. They live in the Atlantic, Pacific, and Indian oceans. They also swim in the Red Sea and the Persian Gulf. In spring, pantropical spotted dolphins **migrate** offshore. In autumn and winter, they move inshore.

SENSES

A dolphin's keen senses are vital to its survival. Spotted dolphins have good eyesight in and out of water. In fact, their eyes move independently. So, they can see ahead and behind at the same time!

Scientists do not believe dolphins have a sense of smell. But, they can taste their food. And, they have a good sense of touch. Their smooth, rubbery skin is very sensitive.

Hearing is another valuable sense. Spotted dolphins listen for the individual whistles they each make. These sounds aid communication.

Hearing is also an important part of echolocation. A dolphin sends out clicks through its **melon**. These sounds bounce off objects in the dolphin's path.

The sounds return to the dolphin as echoes. They give the dolphin much information. The dolphin learns where the object is and how large it is. The dolphin can also tell how fast the object is moving.

Sound wave sent out by dolphin

Echo wave received by dolphin

DEFENSE

Spotted dolphins have several natural predators. Sharks and killer whales threaten both species. Pantropical spotted dolphins face additional enemies. These include false killer whales and pygmy killer whales.

Speed is one defense spotted dolphins have against predators. These powerful animals can swim more than 17 miles per hour (28 km/h). Their excellent sense of hearing helps them listen for danger. And, whistle sounds allow them to communicate warnings.

Humans pose threats that spotted dolphins cannot avoid. Pollution harms dolphins. And in some areas, spotted dolphins are captured for food or bait. They are also caught in fishing nets by accident.

Fishing laws help protect spotted dolphins.
They have lowered the number of dolphins caught
and killed in nets.

*Pantropical spotted dolphins must watch out for
cookie-cutter sharks. These sharks take circular
bites out of their prey!*

FOOD

Atlantic spotted dolphins dig their beaks into the sand to catch hidden fish.

Spotted dolphins often catch their prey near the water's surface. They feed on small fish, including flying fish. They also enjoy eating squid and octopuses.

Some spotted dolphins work together to hunt. Echolocation helps them find their prey. And, they use their whistles to communicate about it.

Spotted dolphins feed on schools of small fish.

Spotted dolphins grasp prey with their cone-shaped teeth. An Atlantic spotted dolphin has as many as 164 teeth. A pantropical spotted dolphin has up to 190! Yet these numerous teeth are not for chewing. Dolphins swallow their prey in one big gulp!

BABIES

After mating, a female pantropical spotted dolphin is **pregnant** for about 11 months. A female Atlantic spotted dolphin is pregnant for about 12 months. Both species almost always carry just one baby at a time. The baby is called a calf.

Calves are born without spots. At birth, a pantropical spotted calf measures up to 33 inches (85 cm) in length. A newborn Atlantic spotted calf is up to 43 inches (110 cm) long. The weight at birth is unknown.

Like other mammals, the mother dolphin makes milk for her calf. Pantropical spotted calves nurse for one to two years. Yet, they start eating solid food after three to six months. Atlantic spotted calves nurse for up to five years.

Male pantropical spotted dolphins live up to 40 years. Females can survive 46 years! Scientists do not know the life span of Atlantic spotted dolphins.

A mother spotted dolphin waits up to four years before having another calf.

BEHAVIORS

Spotted dolphins live together in groups. Near shore, Atlantic spotted dolphins gather in **pods** of 5 to 15. Offshore, groups generally have fewer than

Spotted dolphins frequently leap high above the water's surface.

50 members. But, some include more than 200 dolphins.

Pantropical spotted dolphins will gather in groups of thousands of individuals! These groups consist of smaller **pods** of 10 to 20 dolphins. Members of these smaller groups stay close to one another. They surface and dive at the same time.

Spotted dolphins are acrobats above the water's surface! They leap out of the water and land with a splash. They also like to **bow ride**.

Underwater, Atlantic spotted dolphins are able to dive 200 feet (60 m) deep. They can hold their breath for up to six minutes. Scientists believe pantropical spotted dolphins can stay underwater longer than three minutes. There is still much to learn about these fascinating creatures!

SPOTTED DOLPHIN FACTS

Scientific Names:

Pantropical spotted dolphin *Stenella attenuata*

Atlantic spotted dolphin *Stenella frontalis*

Common Names:

Pantropical spotted dolphin, bridled dolphin

Atlantic spotted dolphin, bridled dolphin

Average Size: Male pantropical spotted dolphins grow five to nine feet (1.6 to 2.6 m) in length. They weigh 198 to 262 pounds (90 to 119 kg). Male Atlantic spotted dolphins measure five to eight feet (1.6 to 2.3 m) long. They weigh 220 to 315 pounds (100 to 143 kg). Females are smaller than males.

Where They're Found: In tropical and warm temperate waters of the Atlantic, Pacific, and Indian oceans

GLOSSARY

bow ride - to swim at the front of a boat or a whale. A dolphin uses the waves created there to assist movement and speed.

cetacean (sih-TAY-shuhn) - a member of the order Cetacea. Mammals such as dolphins, whales, and porpoises are cetaceans.

continental shelf - a shallow, underwater plain forming a continent's border. It ends with a steep slope to the deep ocean floor.

Delphinidae (dehl-FIHN-uh-dee) - the scientific name for the oceanic dolphin family. It includes dolphins that live mostly in salt water.

melon - a rounded structure found in the forehead of some cetaceans.

migrate - to move from one place to another, often to find food.

pod - a group of socially connected dolphins or whales.

pregnant - having one or more babies growing within the body.

temperate - relating to an area where average temperatures range between 50 and 55 degrees Fahrenheit (10 and 13°C).

tropical - relating to an area with an average temperature above 77 degrees Fahrenheit (25°C) where no freezing occurs.

warm-blooded - having a body temperature that is not much affected by surrounding air or water.

WEB SITES

To learn more about spotted dolphins, visit ABDO Publishing Company on the World Wide Web at **www.abdopublishing.com**. Web sites about spotted dolphins are featured on our Book Links page. These links are routinely monitored and updated to provide the most current information available.

INDEX